JOSEF HERMAN
DRAWINGS AND WATERCOLOURS

2 JUNE – 25 JUNE 1995

**Flowers East
at London Fields**

Josef Herman
1911   Born in Warsaw

Recent Selected Exhibitions
1980   *Fourth retrospective exhibition*, Camden Arts Centre, London
Drawings and watercolours, Waddington Galleries, London
Oils, Browse and Darby, London
1981   Awarded an O.B.E. for his services to British art
Terry Dintenfass Gallery, New York
1982   Philip Solomon Gallery, Dublin
1984   Bernard Jacobson Gallery, London
Cyril Gerber Fine Art Gallery, Glasgow
First showing of a substantial group of drawings of West Highland (Skye, Western Isles) fishermen made during 1943
1985   *Drawings and paintings from the Allison Collection*, Pier Arts Centre, Stromness, Orkney
1988   *Drawings and paintings*, 'Wakefield 100' celebrations
Drawings 1944 – 55, Boundary Gallery, London
1989   *Recent works 1984 – 89* and *Homage to the Women of Greenham Common*, Angela Flowers Gallery, London
Paintings and drawings, Beaux Arts, Bath
1990   Elected Royal Academician
Drawings, Boundary Gallery, London
1991   Wakefield Art Gallery and Museum
Watercolours, Flowers East, London
1992   *Retrospective exhibition*, National Museum of Wales, Cardiff
1993   *Recent drawings*, Angela Flowers Gallery, London
1994   *Related Twilights, Fifty years of drawing and painting 1944 – 94*, Boundary Gallery, London
1995   *Drawings and watercolours*, Flowers East at London Fields, London

Public Collections Include
Aberdeen Art Gallery
Arts Council of Great Britain
Atkinson Art Gallery, Southport
Birmingham City Museums and Art Gallery
The British Council
The British Museum, London
Cecil Higgins Museum, Bedford
City Art Gallery, Bristol
The City Art Gallery, Auckland
The Contemporary Arts Society, London and Wales
Durban Art Gallery
Geffrye Museum, London
Glasgow Museums and City Art Gallery
Glynn Vivian Art Gallery, Swansea
Graves Art Gallery, Sheffield
Hamilton Art Gallery, Ontario
Huddersfield Art Gallery
Israel Art Museum, Ein Harod
Jewish Museum, New York
Johannesburg Art Gallery
Kettering Art Gallery
King George VI Art Gallery, Port Elizabeth
Leeds City Art Gallery
Leicestershire Museums, Art Galleries and Record Service
Leipzig Museum der Bildenden Kunste
Manchester City Art Galleries
Melbourne National Gallery
Middlesbrough Art Gallery
Museum of Fine Arts, Montreal
National Gallery of Canada, Ottawa
National Gallery of Queensland, Brisbane
National Gallery of South Australia, Adelaide
National Museum of Wales, Cardiff
Nottingham Art Gallery
Peter Stuyvesant Foundation, Cape Town
Plymouth City Museum and Art Gallery
Rugby Art Gallery
Salford Art Gallery
Scottish National Gallery of Modern Art, Edinburgh
Sheffield City Art Gallery
Southampton Art Gallery
South London Art Gallery
Tate Gallery, London
Tel Aviv Gallery
Toronto Art Gallery, Ontario
Ulster Museum, Belfast
Victoria & Albert Museum, London
Wakefield City Art Gallery
Wellington National Gallery
York City Art Gallery

ALL WORKS ARE ON PAPER
APPROXIMATE SIZE IS 25 x 20 CMS

Flowers East

ANGELA FLOWERS GALLERY PLC
199-205 RICHMOND ROAD
LONDON E8 3NJ

TELEPHONE: 0181-985 3333
FAX: 0181-985 0067

TUESDAY – SUNDAY 10.00AM – 6.00PM

© 1995
JOSEF HERMAN AND FLOWERS EAST

PORTRAIT OF JOSEF HERMAN BY ADRIAN FLOWERS

PHOTOGRAPHY: GARETH WINTERS

CATALOGUE PRINTED BY THE PALE GREEN PRESS

1000 COPIES

ISBN 1 873362 43 9